MY BEAUTIFUL
GREENHOUSE

Audrey Preece

Contents

1. Introduction   1

2. How to: 9

3. Irrigation   33

4. The greenhouse effect on cooling   39

5. The trees   47

6. Tips   55

7. Conclusions   61

Chapter One

Introduction

Glasshouses (also known as greenhouses) and hothouses (also known as greenhouses) are basically structures with roofs and walls created largely of crystalline substances, such as steel, where plants needing controlled climates are grown. They come in diverse shapes and sizes, ranging from tiny spheres to massive monoliths. A chilly stage is the term used to describe a small rainfall. Sunlight warms the inside of a greenhouse even more than the outside, shielding its contents from the chill.

The only thing a greenhouse is, is a means through which plants have been multiplied. These constructions can be either little or extremely huge, depending on the proportions. Roman emperor tiberius required that his fishers guarantee that he had an abysmal cucumber every day, therefore the notion of using a tactic similar to this in current green houses dates back to that period.

Is there a better way to accomplish this?

The greenhouse effect is different when it comes to genuine greenhouses. A greenhouse slows the flow of renewable energy from its own arrangement because it prevents heat that has been spent from escaping through convection from exiting the greenhouse. In order to allow sunshine to pass through the rainwater building's textile, it is made of a mixture of glass and plastic. Because it heats the ground inside the greenhouse, the sun plays a crucial role in the greenhouse's temperature rise. As a result, the greenhouse's atmosphere is warmed by the heated ground, which in turn heats the plants within because of the confines of the greenhouse's design.

global warming's effect on the atmosphere

This is how the greenhouse effect works:

What's the most efficient technique to grow plants?

operating a greenhouse in this manner is the most efficient.

a rationale for constructing a greenhouse

greenhouse operations

To what end does a greenhouse serve?

Greenhouses serve as a barrier between the natural world and the crops you're cultivating, allowing for longer and maybe superior growing seasons. Insects, as well as overheated or cold weather, are protected by these structures. Because of our global climate, the term "greenhouse effect" is more scientific and serious, but for home gardeners, the effect of a greenhouse on plants could actually be beneficial. The idea behind a particular type of greenhouse is to create a space where heat can be maintained. In addition to slowing the flow of renewable energy, the greenhouse's transparent "walls" allow the sun to warm the ground, which in turn raises the temperature of the surrounding atmosphere. An additional cooling system may be used to create an even colder environment for your plants by simply adding a greenhouse to the mix.

As a result of the greenhouse's advantages,

It's a whole inch of fresh produce!

2. Make it easier for people to get their hands on transplants.

A yearly supply of freshly cut blooms

It's a cosy retreat in the dead of winter.

5. The capacity to develop stuff that you wouldn't normally be able to produce (exotic flowers, tropical fresh fruit)

Insects and squirrels will no longer be a problem.

If you want to improve the appearance of a landscape, go all out and do more of what you want to do!

A greenhouse's advantages include the following:

Inch. It may be difficult or expensive to build.

Heater costs might be higher.

Constant monitoring, maintenance, and repair are required.

4. It would raise the cost of water and electricity.

5. It may detract from the garden's aesthetic appeal.

A plastic or glass inflatable garden might seem like an exquisite glass cottage or it can serve a useful purpose. It's up to you how much you want to spend on your inflatable garden. Ultimately, whether or not you decide to buy a greenhouse will rely on whether or not you feel it will improve your quality of life or subtract from it.

Buying a greenhouse? Here's what you need to know and what to avoid.

Before acquiring a greenhouse, here are five things to consider.

Increased variety and testing of plants that were previously thought to be "too fragile"are all possible in a greenhouse. A greenhouse provides a stable atmosphere that protects delicate plants from dangerous weather conditions. The ability to store and germinate our own seeds with rainwater allows us to avoid paying for company start-ups.

The global climate crisis is making its way into your backyard, whether you like it or not. A lack of record breaking snowfalls and "no time before mentioned" fever patterns meant that the only thing we could rely on, especially when it comes to weather, was uncertainty. Climate change is already here, and it's having an impact on every aspect of our lives, including our gardens. You may damage plants, wash away your hard-earned earth, and attract new insects with freak weather systems. It's time for a change in the way you cultivate your plants: a greenhouse protects them from the elements.

With so many greenhouse kits on the market, ranging in size, shape, fabric, and price, it's easy to become lost. The following are some of the most important considerations to make while looking for a greenhouse to suit your gardening needs.

The size of a grower greenhouse is an important consideration.

Tell us about your vision. Perhaps you enjoy gardening in the garden, but are fed up with the lack of diversity and the exorbitant cost of seedlings. Just imagine planting your seeds from scratch amid the warmth and force of your community's spring before it's even begun. If this is the case, a tiny "newcomer" greenhouse may be all that is necessary. To get started, all you need is a futon seat, some earth, and a few seeds.

It's easy to move a cold frame from one garden bed to another to protect young plants from the risk of frost until the weather warms up a bit. Mobile cloches are an excellent way to get a taste of the benefits of a controlled environment, and many fishermen still use their cloches, cold frames, and greenhouses year after year. Their capacity and flexibility are constrained by the fact that they don't require any additional foundation or building permits.

Is it possible to be too big? The "lit'l propagator" has a 4'x4' footprint, whereas the "conservatory" has a 20'x16' footprint, which is large enough to accommodate a commercial performance. The conventional notion is that you should always buy the most expensive greenhouse possible for your site and budget. If you choose the more likely of the two options, you will almost certainly need to go a greater distance. A good question to consider if you have a patio garden is, "Did my garden beds start off this big, or have they grown through the seasons?" Every year, the bulk of us find ourselves pushing the boundaries farther and further. It is more difficult to enlarge a greenhouse, but our love for gardening has a tendency to develop and become more challenging over time.

If the panels become transparent or opaque, what are the alternatives for glazing?

There are three options for a greenhouse lawn: clear, semi-diffused, and opaque. It's up to you how powerful of a light your plants will receive based on these choices.

If your primary goal is to start seedlings for outside transplantation, transparent panels with direct illumination are preferred for seed sprouting. You'll get off to a faster start in life, with more energy and vitality. There is no diffusion in clear glass panels or single-walled polycarbonate, which are both transparent. An easy-to-assemble transparent freshwater greenhouse may be created using Snap & Grow, which is available in a variety of spans and sizes.

In the last stages of a plant's development, however, diffused light is the best option. Like many solexx choices, plants that have a homogeneous cover accomplish optimal photosynthesis and develop up significantly superior contour: more streamlined and balanced rather than towering and leggy from direct illumination. LEDs and fluorescents are two of the most popular lighting options, yet they also have their drawbacks.

What are the frigid months for in terms of insulation and design?

Your garden should be well-insulated if you live in an area where snow and ice are a typical part of the winter landscape and you also want to grow vegetables year-round. Polycarbonate with multiple walls is usually used for this purpose because of the high insulation value provided by the internal air distances (either triple or double) between your layers. In addition to rigid poly carbonate, another great alternative is twin-walled concrete, which delivers a mild, diffused light and an excellent insulating material with additional flexibility. The twin-walled poly-ethylene used in the solexx series of green homes comes in a wide range of sizes and shapes. Another consideration with cold ponds is snow accumulation: make sure the snow load evaluation for the version you're contemplating doesn't put the pond in danger of collapsing during a major blizzard.

Accurate insulation is less important if the winters are light or if the need is for a "season extender" (place to germinate and nurture younger plants in early spring if the outer temperatures are still unknown). Polycarbonate panels with a single layer of tempered glass might be rather good. If you live in a location prone to cold storms or dense storms that produce flying ice or trees, glass may not be the best solution. Yet, polyethelene film is widely utilised as a cheap and straightforward method that provides semi-diffused light; however, the picture's short life cycle and too little strength may be a drawback for some applications. The film can be damaged or ripped by wind, rain, snow, ice, or even falling limbs, and it degrades quickly in the sun. It may look cheap at first, but you must consider the cost and difficulties of replacing the film on a regular basis (every 1 to 6 years). In addition to obtaining a season extender, more insulation will improve the system's performance.

Your online site, your zoning, and your neighbourhood are all examples of logistics and landscape.

Determine the location where your greenhouse will be built and mark it on the map. You can make a close approximation of the décor you're envisioning with string and rebar fragments. Try to imagine how this would affect your outdoor activities, your sightlines, and the views of your neighbours. Choose a greenhouse that appeals to your sense of aesthetics, but also leave room for any landscaping elements that you would like to add around the perimeter. Another option is to use a second building or another combination of trees to provide a wind break in the opposite direction of the prevailing wind, so long as you don't sacrifice too much sun exposure. Consider the amount of time spent in the sun during each season.

Be sure to check up the local zoning restrictions before making any decisions. A rainwater harvesting system may require a permit in some locations, and there may be limits on its size or withdrawal requirements. Even if a smaller greenhouse qualifies as a "shed," it may still be subject to fewer requirements than a larger one because of its smaller size.

An attached greenhouse, or "leanto," may be seen as an improvement and may require additional restrictions and permits. In addition, a greenhouse linked to the home is extremely likely to produce problems with excessive moisture.

5. Standing and service: know who has left the greenhouse. Understand who has departed.

A greenhouse, even a tiny one, is an investment in terms of both money and effort. Do yourself a favour and research the firm that sells and manufactures the greenhouse in advance, or enlist the assistance of someone you can rely on who has already done their homework. Examine the small print and ask yourself a few basic questions:

What kind of guarantee can you count on getting? How many decades and what kind of issues are covered?

Since when and how many kits have been sold by the organisation? With such a large investment, most people want to go with a reputable supplier or manufacturer with a proven track record. An very extended warranty may be of little use if the company goes out of business in the next calendar year.

Exactly how and where would the greenhouse be sent, and how much would the delivery cost? Make sure nothing has been damaged in transit before you start building.

What kind of technical assistance will soon be offered, such as pre-purchase queries, such as aid during setup, or for post troubleshooting? Is the support team available on the weekends?

It is important to know where these items are manufactured and whether or not customer support representatives have firsthand expertise with them.

Members of gardening groups or internet forums can provide beneficial advice. Because they've worked on so many different things, veteran makers are sometimes in a unique position to offer advice on how a particular model will perform as it becomes older.

Preparation is key if you want to expand your ideas about what, when, and how far you can grow in your house. Having the option to grow many of our favourite fruits and veggies in our own backyards is truly a blessing! In many cases, a greenhouse is a crucial building component for completing the gardening seed-to-crop cycle.

With these tips, you can avoid the most common greenhouse blunders.

A minimal amount of labour is required to grow plants in a greenhouse, whether they are ornamental or edible. Make sure to avoid these typical blunders and have a successful growth season.

Humidity

An overabundance of humidity can encourage the growth of mould and other pathogens in your greenhouse, while an underabundance of humidity might cause your plants to succumb to thirst.

Do some research ahead of time on when to plant plants and how much humidity they need. Even if space is at a premium, you may grow them at the same time or create numerous larger greenhouses.

Misting is a great way to increase humidity, but you need to know how much your plants need before you start.

Shade

When it's cold outside, your plants may need a little more colour from the sun. The greenhouse cover raises the temperature inside, so you'll want to apply some sort of plant colouring when the sun is shining directly on it.

Chapter Two

How to:

In addition to DIY stores and Amazon, there are a variety of other shades to choose from. A pulley system or an electrical track and engine system may mechanically remove the colours for you according on how much uv light is absorbed by the greenhouse's roof, or you can manually remove them by pulling them across it. Obviously, this method is going to be more expensive in the future than manual.

Ventilation

The plants will rapidly succumb to infection if there is no air movement. In the winter, if the rainwater does not have any ports, heat will build up within and may nourish your plants.

Automated rainwater venting systems are available from a variety of manufacturers, including ac power (plugged into an external socket) and solar or battery power. You won't have to hurry out and open and close the windows every day.

Heating

Temperatures plummet dramatically at night in the winter. When temperatures fall below freezing in regions like southwest Texas and Florida, greenhouse heaters are the norm.

Don't heat the greenhouse with a regular heater from your residence. They aren't designed for use in a damp or outdoor environment. A greenhouse heater, a patio explosion shield, and outdoor-graded power cable are all you need to get started.

Plants

It is just as important to grow the right plants as it is to grow all the others put together. The "dream list" of plants might help you understand that the only thing you need to grow your own plants is the available space.

Container-bred varieties of commonly grown fruiting plants (such as tomatoes) are worth looking into if you plan to do a lot of container gardening in the future. Bush skillets don't need to be labelled or decorated in any way.

Too-tall plants might lead to an overabundance of plant combing. They are linked to all greenhouse coverings, encouraging the growth of disease, mildew, and mould.

It contains sulfuric acid

In order to acquire a greenhouse, filling containers with shared garden earth is an absolute disgrace. Soil compacts, erasing its beginnings. Even in large pots, the soil at the top dries out when water from the bottom of the container is spilled. The containers became too heavy and cumbersome to carry or move at a steady pace.

You should choose potting soils that do not include garden dirt. Peat moss or coir will always be used to grow plants in hydroponic culture (coconut fiber).

Fertilizers

Before you begin, research your plants' compost and food needs. Conventional "feeds-everything" fertiliser may not meet the needs of plants in a variety of ways. Make sure there is a supply for a lot of plants.

Use a mark system to keep track of each plant's needs, or classify your plants according to how much fertiliser, water, or shade they require. As an example, a plant may appear to need more colour, but its nutrient needs may be different. An identification mark, such as a colourful label or a sticker, lets you know exactly what your plant needs.

It's likely that your greenhouse growing season will be successful and delicious if you plan beforehand.

There are many different types of greenhouses, such as the traditional greenhouse and the polytunnel.

Structures in greenhouses

The type of growth structure used largely dictates the efficacy and develop-ment of a greenhouse's performance. The benefits and drawbacks of each de-sign must be thoroughly studied because there are so many options. Commer-cial greenhouses and the structural elements that make them up are discussed in detail here.

There are several different kinds of green homes.

Generally speaking, three types of green homes exist: lean-tos, detached struc-tures, and structures joined by form and furrow or gutter (chart 1). Because of the proportional restrictions, few lean-to greenhouses are employed for commercial production. Among amateurs, this type of dwelling has become the most popular.

Structure of commercial greenhouses is shown in Graph 1. the gutters are linked, the stancing quonsets are complementing, and there is a lone gable.

Distant from one another, detached greenhouses loom large. However, they are linked to a work area or a hallway where the other greenhouse may be found. Your quonset may be the most common type of submerged greenhouse for commercial manufacturing. Arched rafters are used in the construction of these homes, and the end walls are frequently solid to provide additional support. Quonset greenhouses are suitable for the cultivation of most plants, although the sidewall expansion is limited. Both production and efficiency suffer as a result of this.

At the eave of the ridge and furrow green homes, gutters are used to connect them. Most of the time, an inner wall under the gutter is not a good idea since it limits the effectiveness. Ridge and furrow green homes may be gabled or curved arches, depending on their design. For gabled residences, thick sheeting (glass, fiber-glass) is preferred, but for arched structures, lighter materials are used (i.e. Poly ethylene, polycarbonates). Range refers to a group of connected ridge and furrow greenhouses.

Components of the structure

The primary perpendicular service in a greenhouse would be rafters (chart 2). Two, 34 or 5 ft centres have been the most common locations for them. Rafters can be used as trusses or arches, depending on the greenhouse's diameter. Greenhouses with a width more than 50 feet are often required to have a reinforced truss framework.

In Figure 2, you can see the fundamental greenhouse components: rafter, terminating wall, side pole, side wall, and purlin.

Rafter-to-rafter purlins are horizontal supports that extend along the length of the structure. Depending on the size of the greenhouse, these structural elements are typically set 4 to 8 feet apart. In some cases, purlins may be connected by a cross legged tie. These are helpful in areas where high winds are more common, and may be necessary.

Perpendicular supports, such as those found in negative articles and columns, are typically between one and ten feet in height. This manufacturing area's elevation is determined by these structural components, which have a substantial impact on efficacy. In addition to providing insulation and cooling, side walls can also be opened up.

Materials used to construct the frame

Many different materials might be used to construct green homes. Most common are aluminium, aluminium, and wood and steel. Aluminum is the cheapest and most long-lasting of the three. There are a wide variety of aluminium extrusions available. Rafts and other structural components may then be made using this material.

Because of how quickly it rots in this wet greenhouse atmosphere, wood isn't as popular as it once was. If wood is used, pressure-treated lumber that "resists" rust is preferred. Commercially accessible wood comes in a wide variety of good varieties. The fumes produced by Penta, on the other hand, have been shown to harm plants.

Materials used to conceal

The covers of greenhouses must be transparent enough to allow maximum light transmission while at the same time being durable and cost-effective. Several compounds are created to meet these needs on a commercial basis..

Glass is the finest material for greenhouses since it allows the most light to pass through. However, the structural components needed to support glass are not prohibitively expensive. In addition, the initial investment as well as the necessary upkeep has limited the adoption of glass houses by Texas industrial enterprises. '

Granite is another common concealment material seen in commercial greenhouses and other similar structures. Unlike a traditional glass home, fibre glass does not require the structural components of a glass structure. Ultraviolet (uv) rays, unfortunately, can cause fibre glass to break down. As a result of the swelling of the fibres, transmission efficiency plummets. Depending on the conditions, fibre glass might last as little as five years.

In commercial greenhouses in Texas, double sheets of poly ethylene (pe) image, inflated with air, might be the most common covering. Pe isn't rigid, but it does provide the assistance needed to carry out daily tasks. Generally speaking, a good image may survive around two years before it has to be updated. Due to their minimal initial investment and structural components required to support a specific type of covering, producers have found that this type of material is the most cost-effective for them to produce.

Toddlers now have access to a variety of modern polycarbonate and acrylic products. They may "out function" current chemicals, but there isn't enough research to know for sure.

Compared to aluminium greenhouse frames, these are more attractive.

Once you've decided between aluminium and wood, shop around for the best and most economical greenhouse companies before making your final decision on which model to purchase. This will ensure that you get the best greenhouse for your yard. Wooden greenhouses are also available and popular with fishers, despite the fact that they require more maintenance than their aluminium counterparts.

Greenhouses made of aluminium

Inch. The most essential advantage of aluminium eyeglasses is that they are a quarter to a third of the cost of a greenhouse of the same size.

2. They are also more durable than wooden eyeglasses, especially the most close ones.

Powder-coated choices are available in a variety of colours, including brown, green, blue, and black, so they may easily fit into a garden's colour scheme. Keep in mind that the additional expense of these hues might be as much as a couple hundred pounds. To avoid this, aluminium is a maintenance-free option that turns silver grey.

In order to maximise the amount of light that reaches your plants, aluminium frames have a minimal amount of colour, so the framework is light and easy to install.

To apply bubble vinyl or shade cloth, you'll need high-quality fasteners.

aesthetically pleasing landscapes

Inch. Even the cheapest hardwood greenhouse is more expensive than aluminium, but wood is a more common material that is more likely to be used to maintain a garden.

Even if the wood has been treated, softwoods like price (walnut) are susceptible to rust. Generally speaking, western red cedar may be let to deteriorate into a silver-brown colour. A western red cedar greenhouse is hard to top when it comes to looks. Start searching for manufacturers who provide a rust-proof guarantee.

3. They may be stained in whatever colour you like, or you can simply enjoy the wood's natural colour.

It is straightforward to use pins to attach bubble vinyl or shade cloth to the framework.

5. Choosing a metal foundation is a great option since it will keep the wooden structure from contacting the damp dirt.

A greenhouse or polytunnel

Because of their similar design, both of these designs allow plants to thrive in hotter climates while also allowing plants to survive in cooler ones. In this way, you may be able to produce more and for a longer length of time a wider variety of food (for example, more tropical plants). However, what are the main distinctions between the two?

With galvanised steel hoops and a clear or diffused vinyl coating, polytunnels are constructed. Polytunnels are more economical than greenhouses, but they require a lower initial investment since they are less expensive to build. A simple site clearing is generally all that's needed to get a polytunnel set up on the ground. In addition, they're easier to dismantle, transport, and reassemble than traditional furniture. For twenty years or more, the galvanised steel structure can last, with the polythene normally needing to be changed every seven to ten years. It is possible to customise your polytunnel with a wide range of accessories and modifications to meet your and your plants' specific needs.

Glass or polycarbonate plastic is used to cover an aluminium or alloy structure in a green house. These may be rather pricey, especially if you choose for reinforced safety glass instead (advocated for family homes or gardens with small kids). In addition to taking a long time to construct, green homes are difficult to take down once they have been set up. On the other hand, they are incredibly strong and long-lasting.

Considerations to bear in mind

Consider the following variables when deciding between these two structures and when deciding on the dimensions:

Compared to green houses, polytunnels are more affordable but also demand a larger initial outlay.

Larger greenhouses require more time to construct due to their structural complexity.

Site preparation: a polytunnel may be built on any hard ground, while a greenhouse requires flat, level land.

In comparison to polytunnels, which need to have their covers replaced on a regular basis at a minimal cost in order to maintain their efficiency, green houses may last a lifetime if the glass does not break or blow out of the framework.

A polytunnel coated with weathered polythene and without the vestiges of a rainfall can be useful if you are thinking about over-wintering plants.

Plastic sheeting with diffused light can help keep the polytunnel cool, but it may be necessary to paint rainwater components to prevent sun damage, such as the leaves of a plant being harmed by sunlight.

When it comes to transportability, green homes demand more time and the glass panels might be more dangerous because of the higher risk of injury and damage.

In the end, your decision will most likely come down to a budget and a list of requirements. However, we hope these recommendations will help you choose the best escalating choice for your needs.

Preparation is the key to building a successful greenhouse: choose the appropriate foundation, frame, and glazing for your particular climate and site

A well-designed greenhouse

It is possible to mix use with beauty in a greenhouse. This decision is solely in your hands, as are the resources at your disposal and the scope of your creative vision. Anyone planning to build their own greenhouse should read this tutorial.

It's not hard to see why green homes have become so popular. Using them to produce crops indoors can be expensive, but using them to grow crops outside can save farmers money. If you're looking for a little additional room to grow your favourite plants, this is a great option. It's time to plan a greenhouse!

Creating a greenhouse on your own property will pay off in the long run since you'll be able to enjoy a room full of flourishing plants for years to come. When you're already growing outside, the benefits of adding a greenhouse to your setup to shield your plants from temperature changes, insects, and wind-borne illnesses are obvious.

When purchasing a prefabricated greenhouse from a hardware store, accessories such as chairs, tables, and automated vents, heating, or base equipment are typically not included. This is where it all starts: with thorough planning. You'll need water and power, so think about those circumstances, and be aware of local building limits if you're planning a project that is large enough. There's no reason why you should be forced to change course mid-stream.

To begin, determine the greenhouse's dimensions and placement.

Consider where you'll need help building your greenhouse before you begin designing it. There are a wide variety of green houses to choose from, with a variety of options to meet your area.

When choosing a location for your own greenhouse, consider how much space you will need for ducks, preparation spaces, and storage. Calculating some possible dimensions, keeping in mind that rectangular and square measures aren't the only options. It's possible to utilise a l-shaped greenhouse, or even many tiny green houses, to better organise your space.

Think about where the entrance makes the most sense and how big it should be in the near future. If so, how long will it take to build a path to the farmers? Decide whether or not you want to expand the greenhouse over time.

There are a lot of variables to consider when it comes to the size and materials required for your greenhouse, whether it's a permanent or transportable structure. Finally, if a portion of your greenhouse is located directly across from a wall outlet, keep in mind that this particular side of the greenhouse will not receive as much sun, necessitating additional planning.

evaluating the greenhouse's design

It's also a good idea to take a look at your own personal finances. Before you begin designing the majority of your greenhouse's features, decide how much you're willing to spend. The price per square foot of a greenhouse can vary enormously, ranging from simple hoop constructions to complex timber, glass, and metal buildings with several capacities.

Do you wish to continue cultivating in the cooler months of the year? Your plants will need more insulation and a heating source if this is the case. In order to provide the plants with the light energy they require, are you planning to use a combination of natural solar energy and artificial lighting? It's important to know where and how much artificial lighting is needed in the early phases of your design if this is the case,

The next step is to make a list of the characteristics you value the most and compare it to your budget. Throughout the design process, refer to the record. Adding a vital feature only to discover that it's missing at the end of the design process is a waste of time.

3. The lanes of greenhouses

To obtain your plants, you'll need aisles in your greenhouse. Aisles are more efficient if they've been placed in the middle, which means you may plant from any angle. It's extremely probable that your aisles will become an issue in the future if they don't allow you to easily reach where you're climbing.

Make sure the aisles can accommodate your wheelbarrow, waggon, or handbag trailer if you plan on bringing one. The fundamental layouts of the walls can also play a key role in determining the width of one's aisles.

Aisles that are too close to the walls will make it difficult for people to go through. Hanging baskets are easier to reach in a barn-style greenhouse since they are closer, but the simpler construction and more stable layout means that you must decide where your aisles will run.

In order to plan out your greenhouse's aisles, decide if you can only have one entrance. The number of plants you can grow in your greenhouse is limited by the number of doors you have on the outside of your greenhouse. Another factor to consider is the added expense associated with installing additional doors.

Tables and chairs

Make sure your lanes are reflected in the furniture you choose. To begin, consider the many types of seats and tables that are available and learn about the benefits of each. Remember that water needs to be able to go in and out of your home.

This includes a place to wash your hands and other equipment. Consider multi-purpose tables because these work locations don't truly have room for plants. The only item you'll need to clean your hands or gear is a water-grabbing device.

Please don't put plants on the work table. A dining table's material should consequently be chosen to keep trash from falling on the plants below. Being able to keep a clean and well-organized greenhouse is essential to maximising your yields. There are certain plants that need less sunlight, or even artificial illumination, if chairs or tables are going to block some of them from the sun.

The size and materials of the seats are critical. The low cost of some seats and tables may be enticing, but their design or construction may limit the quantity of direct sunlight that enters the greenhouse. Using barrels to support chairs or tables, for example, may be an option, but this will take up a significant amount of space. It's important to look at all the components of a dining table or chair before making a decision, not just its price. Before committing to a final design, invite the team to reexamine these ideas.

5. The ability to change the design of your greenhouse

As your plants develop or you add more diversity to your mix, you may need to adjust the size or height of your pots. Is the irrigation system flexible enough to accommodate all of these changes? How are artificial lights conveyed or rectified if they are used? In a greenhouse, comfort plays an important role.

Height-adjustable shelves and seats can enhance the design's adaptability, but only if they are built to last. Racks with wheels that aren't simply height-adjustable but also have the right kind of flooring to move around in your greenhouse, allowing you to better utilise your plants, are also an option.

To save on building expenditures while also maximising the amount of light and space available to your most prized plants, consider growing them in flat-rod-suspended hanging baskets. Through the design process, considera-tion should be given to making the most of the sun's rays. Shaded plants don't often yield the best results.

Siding and framing

As soon as you've made up your mind about seating arrangements, tables, hanging sticks, aisles and entryways, think about the materials you'll use for frame and siding. Ceramic, glass, and plastic are just some of the materials available for dental work.

For framing, you can choose from a variety of materials such as wood, alu-minium, stainless steel and vinyl. Before making a decision, learn more about each material's merits and downsides. This amazing item will be influenced by the atmosphere in the community. During the hottest months of the year, might it get too hot? Winters that are bone-chilling? Does your plants require shelter against snow and wind? Choosing the right cladding and frame materials is critical to the long-term viability of your greenhouse.

You'll also want to make sure that the siding is able to let in enough light. How much light enters your greenhouse each day is what actually matters.

It is critical for healthy plant growth that an appropriate supply of photo-synthetically active light be built up. Many gardens are available to help you determine if your plants are receiving the nutrients they need. You can ensure that your plants receive the most amount of sunlight by being able to rapidly wash your siding.

In addition, there are a number of other pieces of equipment

Heating and ventilation or cooling equipment may be necessary in your green-house. Don't forget to include them in your spending plan! Summers in Las Vegas, for example, are tremendously hot, yet the air remains dry. For both you and your plants, an evaporative cooler in a dry environment may do wonders for both parties, reducing stress levels to the absolute minimum. When growing plants that don't require a lot of direct sunlight, shade cloth might be an asset.

It should be a lot of fun to plan for a new greenhouse. You'll get more enjoyment out of your greenhouse once it's finished if you put more thought into it and enjoy the planning process. From the standpoint of maximising profits, the advantages of a well-designed greenhouse cannot be overlooked.

Creating a system for your greenhouse

deciding on a floor's appearance

Pea-gravel and flooring specifically built for green homes are the finest options for floors. Even while the floor helps keep weeds out, the pea gravel can allow for adequate drainage. In the case of disease, both may be easily disinfected with a moderate bleach solution.

For greenhouse flooring, how may this material be used?

There are a wide variety of hardwood floor materials to choose from. When it comes to the ideal floor, poured concrete is the best option. Concrete floors are easy to clean and walk on, and if pumped correctly, should drain any excess water. During the day, concrete may reflect light and keep heat in. However, pouring concrete isn't the only option if you want to catch rainfall on your lawn. There are a variety of greenhouse floor ideas available, each with its own benefits and drawbacks. Decide what benefits a hardwood floor has for you before putting in a foundation. It's important to think about how long you'll be spending in the greenhouse, as well as how long particular flooring materials last. Concrete, on the other hand, can last for decades, but a mulch floor degrades rapidly. Your financial strategy is also important to keep in mind.

There are a few things to keep in mind when it comes to the greenhouse floor:

Inch. Crushed rock or gravel mixed with bud cloth can be used as a basis for a greenhouse. This flooring is easy to install, easy to clean, and relatively affordable.

For a chic greenhouse floor, consider lava and landscape stone. While neither lava nor landscape stone is difficult to clean, lava illuminates water and helps to the overall warmth level. These are simple materials, yet they can be expensive at times.

When it comes to green house flooring, mulch may be the least helpful option. A cheap option is not washable and contains fungus and germs when it's cheap. Besides that, it breaks down quickly.

The greenhouse's humidity is increased thanks to the bricks. To improve drainage and stability, they should be encased in a layer of sand. In the same fashion, a sand-coated stone base should be used. Clay flooring are another choice that is both long-lasting and easy to walk on.

A great option for greenhouse floors has been marijuana mats, which can be found in commercial greenhouses. Insect and weed barriers may be readily extended and stapled into place.

Because of their ease of cleaning and excellent drainage, specialty greenhouse vinyl tiles are becoming increasingly popular. They may be used as a course or as part of an entire foundation.

Various types of greenhouse flooring can be used for this purpose, as long as they are easy to clean and drain properly. Put in a bud mat obstacle atop snowy gravel or dirt in the event that you decide to omit a poured concrete base. Place old rubber or carpet mats in areas where you'll be working for long periods of time if you opt to go with a concrete foundation.

The greenhouse catalog's green houses require very little internet preparation. To get the best results, just level the area where the greenhouse will be placed. Each of the green houses you will see has a basis of some kind, so there is no need for a long-term foundation. These pointers, when combined with your greenhouse design, can result in the ideal set-up.

Choosing a place to go

Place your greenhouse in a region that gets a lot of sunshine. As a precaution, if you're concerned about attracting too many visitors to your greenhouse during the sweltering summer months, you may want to situate it in a location that receives some shade throughout the day. Try to keep the greenhouse away from other potential dangers, such as falling tree limbs.

In order to get the most out of your own greenhouse, it's important to know what you plan on using it for. At least six hours of sunlight each day is required if your goal is to grow plants to maturity or to continue cultivating them throughout the fall and winter. It sounds much more difficult than it actually is.

Your initial choice should be a location to the south or south southeast of your home or other structure, which will receive the most sunlight. A location to the east of any buildings is the next best option, since it will receive the majority of the sun from November through February. Because the plants are dependent on the amount of sunshine, the north of a home may not be ideal. You'll need to offer more heat and light.

Keep in mind that the angle of the sun's rays is much lower in the winter than it is in the summer. Due to extended shadows cast by citrus and construction trees, the sun's rays may be partially obstructed in the winter.

To acquire cuttings for propagation, start with seedlings and transplants, then locate a somewhat shaded region. Adding a colour cloth may help reduce the amount of light that enters the greenhouse if an adequate one is unavailable. The following strategy involves burying your waters behind deciduous trees to provide shade from the hot summer sun, while also increasing its exposure to winter light. In this climate, the greenhouse, especially if it has a glass roof, runs the danger of being damaged by shrinking tree limbs.

Many people are curious as to the greenhouse's orientation, or more specifically, the way it faces. The north/south management appears to be preferred by commercial farmers because it gives a constant supply of sunlight. There's new evidence to suggest that the optimum management practises are dependant on your own latitude; for example, an east/west European orientation is preferable when you're above 40 degrees of latitude. When the greenhouse door is opened, cold air will enter, so make sure the entry is always facing away from the prevailing winds to minimise heat loss.

laying the groundwork

A lot of people feel that a concrete or brick foundation is the best option for a greenhouse floor. In fact, even in a greenhouse, such floors can be a source of illness and mould growth. In addition, these bases take a lot of time and money to build, so they're not for everyone. In order to move your greenhouse in the event that you need to, you'll need a simpler floor choice. If you decide to build a permanent basis, it may be more efficient to build a greenhouse first and then expand the base to the desired dimensions. People are sometimes surprised to find that the green houses they built don't match the foundation they put in.

The optimal foundation for a greenhouse is a concrete slab.

Before you begin building your own greenhouse, you must decide on the type of greenhouse base you will use to support it. You may have a few options when it comes to the materials you use, but it's imperative that you see all of them so that you can choose the best one for your area and the greenhouse you're building.

Is it there to stay or is it just a matter of time

It's important to consider if you intend to move the greenhouse in the near future or whether you intend to keep it as a permanent part of your property. In many cases, homeowners who want to produce their own plants or veggies may ask you to remove the greenhouse if they ever decide to sell their home. Most of the time, these types of greenhouses are more compact and easier to construct than other varieties. Because they are just temporary, you will need a base that can sustain the greenhouse's weight yet is easy to remove when the time comes. This type of application can benefit from a basic wooden base, which is also a low-cost choice that makes it simple to move your DIY greenhouse to a new location whenever necessary.

If you want to build a larger greenhouse or live in an area with particularly harsh winters, you may want to consider a much more solid foundation. It is possible to build a greenhouse of any shape or size using a poured concrete base, which is a far more durable option. The base for your greenhouse should be buried deep into the ground around the building's perimeter. Using this type of base might extend the life of your greenhouse, since it is quite durable. While a concrete basis is a little more work than other options, it's well worth the effort for the additional years that it allows for your personal construction. Concrete offers all the support and anchoring strength your greenhouse needs after it has been constructed.

It's also possible to use a beam and post base, a combination of the previous two options. Rather of following the perimeter of this structure, its base relies on a number of different objects for support. In most greenhouses, these poles are made of either treated or concrete lumber and are buried below the frost level in the perimeter of the greenhouse. Later on, these items will be used to support the beams that make up the greenhouse's base. A column and post solution, in contrast to other foundations, actually improves the soil arrangement marginally. A base like this is ideal for any size greenhouse, but it's also easy to shift about if you need to. With only a little digging, the poles could be removed, restoring the area to its previous form. In windy areas, this type of base provides a more secure anchor for some DIY rainfall than a more conventional timber structure. By burying the poles, rainfall is kept more firmly in place and the minimal movement that can occur with a conventional wooden basis is reduced or eliminated.

For inspiration, go through your greenhouse plans.

Many greenhouse plans define the optimum basis for the model you're creating, which may be a huge help in making the right decision. In addition, you should take into account where you live in the nation. If you live somewhere where the winters are harsh, you'll want to build a foundation that can survive the shifting of the frozen ground. In most cases, this means placing the base below the freezing point of the water in the reservoir. This ensures that when the earth freezes, the building above it will not twist or shift.

The greenhouse's stability is also dependent on the strength of your foundation. Your homemade rainwater will be exposed to the elements and must be firmly secured to the foundation in order to survive wind and rain. Using a base that can provide this anchoring is vital to getting the most out of one's new greenhouse and also giving the support it needs for a long time in the future.

Determine the optimal greenhouse length

A greenhouse's framing is sometimes overshadowed by the siding, but if the framing is made of a weak or unstable material, the structure won't stand the test of time. It's difficult to build a greenhouse until the initial frame is properly built, and even if you do, you'll realise later that it has gaps and crevices that make it difficult to keep out insects and other small critters and draughts.

With a custom greenhouse, you have the option of choosing what materials to use to create the framework, whereas some greenhouses are provided in kit form and don't give you these options. Here are some things to keep in mind while considering the four most common greenhouse materials: aluminium, wood, stainless steel, and pvc vinyl pipe.

Wood

Wood is a beautiful material that may be used to create a classic greenhouse design. However, unless you're creating anything more akin to a garden or sunroom storage shed, using lumber as the framework for a greenhouse is quite impractical. Wood is an excellent insulator, and it's easy to make and attach to a structure. As a result, many timbers will harden and rust in a greenhouse due to the constant presence of damp conditions. If you decide to utilise wood, go with a species like cedar or redwood that is well-known for its resistance to moisture and rust. Or, if you like, choose chemically treated wood that is designed for outdoor use. Using a loofah every few years will help you live longer, no matter what kind of wood you're using.

Due to its own solar panels, wood is an ideal material for greenhouses that will employ polycarbonate.

Aluminum

Due to its resistance to corrosion and breakdown, aluminium is one of the most low-maintenance building materials available. For greenhouse frameworks, the service members must be made of heavy-gauge aluminium or pitched up, as aluminium is not as durable as steel. However, for freshwater or glass panels, aluminium provides an ideal rigid shape. Any colour you can think of may be achieved by painting or anodizing aluminium.

Zinc-coated steel

Galvanized steel is a cost-effective option for long-term durability. Your greenhouse will generally require fewer framing colleagues, which means that fewer beams will have to be cast into it. Polyethylene film is used in conjunction with steel frames rather than solid glass or solid panels. Commercial growers prefer greenhouses with galvanised metal frames and plastic picture coverings, but they may not be so appealing in a domestic environment. The galvanising will eventually wear off and the steel will rust, which is a huge downside for stainless steel.

vinyl pipe made of PVC

Pvc plastic pipes are inexpensive, light, and easy to make. Despite the fact that a pvc framework is not as strong as a wooden one, it may be used as a cover for designs that include metal supports. As a plus, PVC frame allows less heat loss than aluminium. Polyethylene picture is always used as a wall covering in pvc-framed green homes. For a large greenhouse, vinyl pipe isn't a good option; they are often hobby-sized garden greenhouses. PVC frames are now standard in most hobby green houses available as kits.

Everything you'll need to create a greenhouse at home.

Ten simple steps to building a greenhouse

The first step is to select a greenhouse design / frame.

To meet your needs, we provide a wide choice of greenhouse configurations in various styles and sizes. A greenhouse's overall efficiency and functionality will be determined by this step, which is one of the most critical in the construction process. Each inflatable arrangement is specifically designed for a variety of uses and may be put to good use in many different ways. Investigate the features and benefits offered by each greenhouse type described on our greenhouse string pages, then consult our buying a greenhouse guide to make a final decision that best suits your needs and budget. When you have further questions or can't decide on a greenhouse structure, contact us and we'll help you design your greenhouse project.

Second, hardware and doors are examined.

When planning a rimol greenhouse construction, keep in mind that you'll need access and exit methods that are both functional and in keeping with the aesthetic you're aiming for. You're sure to discover just what you're looking for with your most do or alternatives in a variety of distinctive colours and sizes. You can rely on our grade doors to endure for a long time, and they're well-insulated to keep the rainfall from escaping. Having all of these doors will make it easy to enter inside your greenhouse at all times.

Another critical stage in building a greenhouse is deciding on the hardware that will hold it all together. You must ensure that the nuts, bolts, and mounts you use in your rainwater collection systems are sturdy enough to withstand the hardest weather conditions.

The third step is to select a covering.

Choosing the right cover for your greenhouse is an essential step in creating an ideal growth environment. You may select the perfect covering for your needs and budget by choosing from a variety of materials and thicknesses offered by green homes. Wind and snow won't rip or damage these covers, which are robust and long-lasting. To protect your rainwater collection system and keep you going for a long time, you may rely on weapons from greenhouse systems. Once you've chosen your covering, be sure to check out our instructions for installing and covering a polycarbonate rainwater collection system.

Heating and heating as a fourth measure

Ventilation is a common worry when individuals inquire about greenhouse construction. To keep your plants from overheating, you must have a way to cool your greenhouse. A variety of heating solutions are available, including mechanical ventilation, natural ventilation, and sealing. Whatever method you choose to employ to cool your greenhouse, we have a wide range of high-quality services and equipment that will meet your needs in an efficient and effective manner. You may check over our greenhouse options for heating and ventilation to see which one best suits your needs. Our guide on sizing fans and dividers will help you figure exactly how much cooling you'll need for your greenhouse.

Select a heating system for your property in step 5.

As part of your rainwater harvesting strategy, you should also add warmth for your plants. Propane and propane heaters, gas heaters, convection tubes, hot water heaters, and many more are among the heating options we offer to meet the needs of all types of growers. We have everything you need for practically every greenhouse heating system application you can imagine. Using our instructions on how to build a home heating, select the heating system that is most suited to the greenhouse construction and then determine the desired size.

Environmental controls are the sixth step.

Controlling the hvac system is critical for building a greenhouse that is both practical and energy efficient. We provide a wide range of environmental control options for every type of grower, ranging from simple toaster techniques to more powerful computer modules. You won't ever get upset or confused with these controllers since they are so easy to use and understand. Your greenhouse may rely on our expertise to provide an ideal growth environment for your crops. Check out our in-depth post on medical management programmes to learn more about their benefits and features.

Step 7: Addition of new devices

Nov-ices Researching how to create a greenhouse necessitates a thorough examination of all of the systems involved in establishing a fully functional greenhouse. Plants may benefit from a co2 generator's increased production. Your plants will always be properly ventilated with a simple watering technique. It is possible to create a successful and effective ascending environment in a limited space using a variety of different technologies.

Benching is the eighth and last step in the process.

Applications are an important component of making your greenhouse building perform the way you want it to. Our seats are available in a wide range of materials, sizes, and designs, allowing you to find exactly what you're looking for. Those chairs, which are made of heavy-duty steel, will last for a very long time. Call us and we'll help you find the most chairs that you desire. We can make just about any custom seat you choose.

How to purchase a greenhouse on your own

In the event that you've completed your greenhouse plans, as well as any further accessories, it's time to determine the layout. Check our terms and conditions to make sure you understand the ordering process before filling out a couple of our quotation request forms. Once you've sent your order, we'll do all we can to deliver it to you as soon as possible.

Build your greenhouse as the tenth step.

You must now build your greenhouse's construction after acquiring all of the necessary equipment. There are a number of instructional guides and data sheets available to help you build your own greenhouse, even if it initially appears to be a daunting task. Please get in touch with us right away and we'll send you a PDF of any documents you need. Be sure to obtain a building permit from the local government and to be familiar with the structure and taxation of your own building before starting your project. If you have any additional questions or concerns during the construction process, don't hesitate to contact us! We'll be happy to help you out!

A greenhouse's construction procedure

If you've ever wanted to grow your own flowers and vegetables in a greenhouse in your backyard, you're not alone. Having a greenhouse allows you to get a head start on spring pruning and extend the growth season into the fall, as well.

Prior to making a decision on a greenhouse, there are a number of things to keep in mind. Like:

Ordinances of the locality

Get permission from your city's building department to establish a rainwater collection system on your own property. Because green homes are often regarded as out-buildings, you'll have to submit an application for a building permit. Because most home communities have severe no-outbuildings covenants, obtaining the consent of the hoa may be challenging, especially if you live in a neighbourhood with an employer's association (hoa).

Orientation toward the sun

Because a greenhouse's purpose is to provide your plants with a warm, light environment, it is critical that you locate it appropriately in your yard. In order to catch the early morning sun, it is best to fly your drone facing south or south east. Many ponds might benefit from an east-facing position, as well.

Try to pick a location that gets at least half an hour of continuous sunlight every day. If you live in an area that sees a lot of snowfall, be sure that the greenhouse's snow load evaluation can support a layer of snow without the snow ever accumulating.

Alternatives to glazing

When it comes to glazing for green homes, glass is the most common option. There are several advantages to using polycarbonate or polyethylene sheets instead of glass, but they are more expensive and more difficult to work with.

Even though fibre glass might discolour over time, polycarbonate, acrylic, and fibreglass are resilient, excellent insulators, and exceptionally good light transmittance materials. Although polyethylene sheeting is inexpensive and easy to install, it is not very robust and may easily be ripped and damaged.

Frames are made of many materials.

Metal and wood are the two most common materials used to build greenhouses' frame. For small to medium-sized greenhouses, wood is a more cost-effective and more easy material to employ. Aside from the higher cost, steel is more robust and weather-resistant than lumber. Aluminum is a great material to use because of its light weight, resistance to corrosion, and sturdiness.

Materials for the floor

The floor of a rainwater can be made from a variety of materials, including wood, gravel, flagstone, metal grates, poured concrete, or bare earth. Remember, though, that if your yard remains bonedry, a dirt ground is a viable option. Otherwise, it will become a muddy bog.

Although concrete is extremely long-lasting, it is also highly expensive to pour and does not drain well. An inexpensive, draining cave floor may be resurfaced by simply adding soil.

The law on personal injury

Temperature modulation in the greenhouse is essential since it can turn stiflingly hot or severely cold at any time of year. Exhaust fans and movable windows can help restore a warm atmosphere. Utilize dark-colored materials to reduce the absorption of solar heat.

Install a gas heater with a thermostatically controlled fan to keep the greenhouse warm when the weather turns chilly. Passive solar panels may be useful in warm areas. For a greenhouse, pile barrels or concrete blocks on top of each other and let them soak up solar rays throughout the day so they may be released as heat at night.

Environment of a greenhouse, including irrigation system, ventilation, lighting, humidity and temperature gauges, and air conditioning.

Because the conditions in the greenhouse are engineered to bring crop performance as close as possible to its inherent best, growers reap the greatest possible benefits from the setup. In order for the plant to transform sunlight, water, carbon dioxide, and minerals into a product that can be sold, a rainwater collection system was developed. Therefore, the protected environment of the greenhouse generates a "comfortable" climate amid the hostile environment. If you already have a comfortable environment, there is no reason to spend more money on a more expensive smaller comfortable climate just for the purpose of cultivating plants.

Before the invention of greenhouses, the food that we ate on a daily basis was highly dependent on the seasons. If you lacked the financial means to purchase non-perishable goods, your only option was to consume fish that had been caught from a variety of ponds. More plants can be enhanced across the board now that a more secure environment has been developed.

The major purpose of a greenhouse is to maintain a consistent temperature and level of humidity within. In most cases, problems with the design and location of green houses are the source of an unlimited number of temperature and humidity-related concerns. A greenhouse that has been thoughtfully planned should be able to provide the appropriate plants with the ideal atmosphere to get returns in a period of time that will make this type of installation economically viable. Do not fall into the trap of believing that a greenhouse can solve all of your problems because although it may solve one issue, it will likely bring up a whole new set of issues that need to be managed. This is basically the point where the majority of beginning players make a serious error. The conditions that are ideal for a plant's development also benefit microorganisms and insects, which means that same conditions are not ideal for plants.

The following are the ecological aspects of greenhouses that are most important:

a method of watering crops

· ventilation

· humidity

contamination

illumination

a calming effect

Chapter Three

Irrigation

Irrigation is a method in agriculture that involves applying water to plants at specific times and in specific amounts to achieve optimal growth. When water and plants are combined, the plants receive some of the essential nutrients that are necessary for the process of photosynthesis to take place.

The process known as photosynthesis is the means through which plants generate their own nourishment. In order for a plant to complete the process of photosynthesis, it needs a variety of different things. One of these items is carbon dioxide (CO_2), and the plant also needs water. When these components are taken into a plant, light will activate chemical processes that take place in structures within the plant cell known as chloroplasts. These reactions will ultimately lead to the production of glucose, which will provide the plant with a source of energy. Just at that same instant, oxygen is also released into the air for all of us to benefit from.

This process of photosynthesis cannot proceed without the presence of water. Because of this, it is of the utmost importance to have a greenhouse that is operational in order to set up an effective irrigation programme that will supply you with the optimal quantity of water for its harvest at the suitable times and in the appropriate quantities.

It may sound confusing, but drip irrigation is just irrigation that is managed to a harvest using dripper technology. Every one of our plants has its own one-of-a-kind dripper tubing, which is usually inserted into the trunk of the substrate block where they are sitting. It is also crucial to ensure that the dripper is not driven into the block with an excessive amount of force, since this makes it a great deal less difficult for the plant roots to have access to the nutrient-rich water.

Ventilation

Ventilation is utilised to either lower the temperature inside of the greenhouse or bring the relative humidity level down. Both forced and natural forms of ventilation are available. Natural ventilation is frequently the very first stage in the heating process since it is easy to implement and costs very little. The majority of manufacturers make an effort to combine many different methods of venting, such as using powered ventilation in conjunction with fans. The climate is more uniform, and the returns of most of the plants are more equally matched, when there is adequate internal flow. The heating component of the pan and fan process is far more important than the ventilation component.

Few farmers put much thought into the question of whether or not naturally ventilating their buildings is effective. Nevertheless, it is of utmost significance. The cost of your greenhouse's cooling system will be decreased to some degree if it has a high level of efficiency in heating down the greenhouse itself. When it's likely to happen, then the angle at which this greenhouse is located in relation to the current winds may also aid with the ventilation efficiency. The greenhouse may produce hot air from its vents as a result of the sucking action of air moving across their surface, as well as a warmer and more humid climate in its lower regions.

The relative humidity inside of a greenhouse

In the same way as fever does, humidity plays an important part in the growth of the harvest. Restoring humidity is often a talent that is required since it in-fluences in the opposite direction you would like it to when you are attempting to control the temperature. For example, if you lower the temperature and increase the ventilation rate, you can often reduce the amount of humidity in the air. This may not be the best outcome, particularly when dealing with cucumbers, which require a rather high relative humidity in the environment. All contemporary greenhouses are designed to have an airtight seal (wellas far as you possibly can). When compared to conventional greenhouses, the rela-tive humidity found inside of modern green houses that have been insulated is significantly greater. Therefore, with green houses having a higher efficacy, there is a need for improved management and control in order to achieve optimal temperature and humidity regulation.

What exactly causes fluctuations in the greenhouse's humidity is the question.

Let's start with the plants themselves. A significant amount of the water needed for plants to survive is lost through evaporation. A cucumber plant can use up to 3 litres of water each day. 95 percent of this water is used to regulate its internal temperature, while the remaining 5 percent is put to use in metabolic processes. All of the water has been sprayed into the greenhouse, which adds to the overall humidity in the environment. When compared to crops that produce a smaller yield, such as lettuce, cucumbers have a much larger leaf area index (lai) for the transformation process. In comparison to huge leafy plants, smaller plants are likely to have a less impact on the greenhouse's overall level of humidity as it builds up.

Temperature as well as the atmosphere within the greenhouse

The first need or purpose of green houses is to maintain normal temperatures, which allows plants to be cultivated even in colder locations than would otherwise be possible. The difference in temperature between the inside of the greenhouse and the outside has simply been limited by the total amount of energy that can be used for the heating system. This particular wavelength shifts from roughly 340-374 nm to 3550-25,000 nm throughout the course of the day, which is what causes the sun to produce its natural heat. The short wavelengths permeate the greenhouse, and their wave lengths shift as a result of interaction with the many objects inside it. Because the very long wavelength rays are unable to pass through the rainfall, they are responsible for warming the air within the building. This is the most straightforward method of straightforward heating. Because of this, the temperature within a greenhouse will most likely quickly exceed the temperature outside, even if it is subzero outside. This is the case even if the greenhouse is not heated.

The material that is utilised to pay for the greenhouse will determine the disparity in temperature that will be applied. Nevertheless, I'm not going to be talking about fans and vents. The temperatures in the centre of the greenhouse, also known as the atrium, will be higher than those on the greenhouse's edges. This is only possible due to the fact that the holes or boundaries of the area prevent air flow from proceeding toward the centre. In all appearances, the core becomes unmoving.

They have been able to lower the temperature inside than it is outside thanks to the introduction of green homes that are better built, taller, and constructed. In Africa, there would have been an infinite number of greenhouse freezers if but for the fact that space is limited. In most cases, while using open technology, the temperature difference between the inside and the outside of the greenhouse won't be much more than 7 degrees Celsius when you are trying to reduce the temperature in the greenhouse.

If we do not utilise vents, fans, doors, or pads to regulate the heat within the greenhouse, then the following will have an influence on the temperature both during the day and at night within the greenhouse:

sort of harvest: why is it a little crop like quickly growing lettuce or apples, and why does it climb up high? Although they require less light from the sun, larger plants, little plants allow for greater air flow throughout the greenhouse. Plants that have a higher leaf area are able to soak up more sunlight, which causes them to generate more heat during the evening. The circulation of air is slowed down by the presence of massive plants.

what exactly is the density of those leaves, which take up the quantity that is below the greenhouse gas? Small compact leaves, such as pops and brinjals, like a tremendous quantity of leaves going high up in the plant.

what kind of material might possibly be used to cover the ground? The darker the fabric, the longer it takes for heat or light to be consumed, which will shortly be emptied out at night, making the inflatable warmer during the day. White chemicals deflect the sun's rays in such a manner that the plant can still utilise them for photosynthesis, but they also change the way the light seems to the plant. The question is, therefore, whether it is heat or light that you seek. The challenge for your grower will be to strike a healthy and sustainable balance between the two. Even if you are only able to heat the greenhouse with the sun a little bit during the colder months, you will still save money on your heating bill. Unfortunately, cold weather is associated with lower levels of sunlight, and since photosynthesis requires more of a chemical that emits light, this presents a problem. It is a dilemma that almost all farmers have, and it is one that you will need to find a solution to during the course of your farming career.

Because it controls the amount of sunlight that reaches the surface, the ozone layer in greenhouses has a significant effect on the temperature. The more opaque the covering, the more the light is affected. It is not required that the very best be made of transparent materials like glass. Some type of diffusion will aid to increase the photosynthetically active radiation that is received by the plant, which will ultimately result in the plant's increased growth.

the latitude at which you are now located as well as the angle of this property. It has to do with the angle at which the sun hits any surface in your tube, along with the cladding, and how they interact. When the sun's rays hit your ground at an angle of 90 degrees, they will likely be stronger than when they strike it at an angle of 20 degrees. At this point, it should be obvious that the seasons of winter and summer are introduced, should they not be?

The key component that has an effect on the size of the crop is stress. There are many varieties of plants, each of which thrives best in a specific temperature range, and as a result, there are many distinct phases of plant development. In the end, it all boils down to a question of direction and payment. It is impossible for it to be flawless at this point in time. It is necessary for the greenhouse to be capable of maintaining an inside temperature that is, on average, between 15 and 30 degrees Celsius, regardless of the temperature outside. There is a good chance that the product selection may shift slightly in the direction of a greater emphasis on tropical plants like tomatoes, cucumbers, and peppers, and a decreased emphasis on lettuce, broccoli, spinach, and a number of other herbs. The fact that the harvest has to be protected from temperature extremes that create stress and diminish return is the reason why rainwater is necessary for this purpose.

There is a great deal more work involved in lighting a greenhouse than first appears. When looking for the optimal lighting for their greenhouse, growers need to take into consideration not only the type of crop being grown, but also the time of year, as well as the amount of sunlight that is available.

In general, green houses need a half an hour of daily lighting that is either a complete spectrum or guide spectrum. In the event that this cannot be accomplished organically, it will be necessary to introduce more light. For the purpose of enhancing crop development and yield, supplemental lighting would involve the use of several artificial lights of a high intensity. Hobbyists are more likely to make use of them in order to maintain growth and expand the grow, whilst commercial growers prefer to make use of these in order to increase earnings and yields.

The photoperiod control light is an extremely important component that should not be overlooked. A plant's photoperiod may be defined as the span of hours during which it is exposed to light at intervals ranging from two to four hours. For illustration purposes, a photoperiod of 14 hours has elapsed when the sun rises at six in the morning and sets at eight in the evening every day. Photoperiod control lights have traditionally been used to simulate lengthy days, which either encourages delayed blooming or triggers early flowering, depending on the requirements of the plant being grown.

Growers have access to a vast range of lighting options; hence, it is essential to have a solid foundational understanding of the fundamentals behind a variety of lighting strategies. Let's have a look at the benefits and applications of the four different kinds of light.

Chapter Four

The greenhouse effect on cooling

Greenhouses frequently necessitate the installation of heating systems. This occurs if the daily average temperature is high enough for your plants to be stressed, preventing them from functioning to their full potential. In circumstances such as this one, heating is the one and only option for continuing to maintain the plants' health and productivity within the building. Heating an indoor space is less expensive than heating a greenhouse. Because of this, putting money into a cooling system has to be one of the most common options.

A method that uses an underfloor heating system is the most efficient way to collect rainwater. Evaporative cooling is the process of causing little amounts of water to evaporate, which results in a reduction in temperature even when there is an increase in the amount of humidity present.

There are only two systems, high-pressure and the pad and fan cooling system, that utilise this idea in commercial greenhouses. Both of these methods involve chilling the plant's leaves. In recent decades, semi-closed greenhouses have been constructed according to the exact same basics as the pad and fan system.

Cooling with pads and fans

Because of how simple it is to use, the pad and fan cooling system is one of the most common types of cooling systems. It makes use of both ventilators and wet pads, as suggested by the name of the product. This greenhouse is equipped with a couple of blowers that expel air, which creates a vacuum-like effect all over the greenhouse. Pad-walls that have the capability of being kept wet are erected on the opposite sides of the buffs. Because of the suction movement that is caused by the buffs, heated air from the outside is sucked into the greenhouse whenever the wet pads are in use. The water that is absorbed by the pads evaporates into the atmosphere, which results in an increase in the environment's humidity but a decrease in its temperature.

Fogging caused by high pressure.

Higher pressure fogging works to the primary of the underfloor heating system in the same way that the pad and fan system does. An extremely small hole was used to funnel water into one of the nozzles, which raises questions about the legitimacy of the operation. The formation of fog results mostly from the fragmentation of water into extremely minute particles. These heated water particles have been absorbed into the surrounding environment before they impact on the exit of their harvest, but only when the temperatures and humidity levels within the greenhouse have made it possible for this to happen. In the same manner as with the pad and fan, the level of humidity has greatly increased, and the temperature in the greenhouse has decreased.

a greenhouse with some open sides

In order to facilitate the development of this semi-closed greenhouse, we are making use of not one but two pads and fans, in addition to rigorous fogging. The manner in which cold air is brought into the greenhouse may be the aspect that stands out as the most significant difference. Greenhouses that are only partially closed make use of a structure known as a climate room. In this chamber, the air may be heated or cooled as needed. This medicated air is blasted off by big ventilators into the greenhouse at polyethylene tubes located underneath the hanging gutters.

How to protect your greenhouse from being damaged by the wind

As soon as the end is inside the greenhouse, it is going to do all in its power to find a way to escape again. It departs in precisely the same manner in which it arrived. As more air is directed from the source, the pressure increases until there is an absolute necessity for something to deliver. The glazing clamps have come loose, and the panes have been removed.

Replace any panes of glass that have been removed from the window that are missing as soon as it is practical to do so. This will reduce the number of breezes that are able to gain access. The majority of skilled glazing enterprises keep conventional sizes of horticultural glass in store; however, if you require odd sizes or want toughened glass or polycarbonate, you may have to order it. It is possible to make a temporary repair to leaking glazing by using glazing repair tape; however, it is best to replace it as soon as possible because the patch may break during more heavy drainage or under snow.

When I was installing my fresh new glass panes, I awoke to find w-clips (the individuals who hold the glass into the framework) everywhere around; the number of clips that initially included the rainfall was nowhere near! In order to provide the glazing clips with an additional layer of durability, cosmetic sheeting is applied in the attachment process.

There is a possibility that some green houses will have pub caps installed so that the panes may be carried inside. Since they are the most reliable choice, it is important to determine whether or not they were intended to be used with the specific model in question. Unfortunately, they are not designed to work with my greenhouse, so I had to use glazing fixing tape to secure each pair of panes, both inside and outside, because this looked to be the area that was failing.

A breeze is able to enter via even the tiniest of breaches in a framework, which is why it is essential to cover up any openings that may exist. It's possible that if you look really closely, you'll see that the framework doesn't quite fit together completely at the corners or at the end of this ridge. Due to the fact that it was all I had on hand, I patched the holes with tape both inside and outside; nevertheless, silicone sealer would have been a far more long-lasting option.

If your greenhouse has a lock catch, check to see that it keeps the door shut extremely securely at all times. In any other case, you may stop it from blowing up by constructing a solid brick masonry wall against it.

Check the condition of the rubber gas strips and clogs that are located across the entryway, the windows, and the various ports, and replace them if they are in poor condition. Windows and vents need to have a secure closing. I've found that applying a strip of polyurethane anti-hotspot tape (intended for use in batting cages) over the framework of my greenhouse roof window port not only gives it a much better seal but also stops it from rattling at the end. This tape is developed for use in batting cages.

It is possible for a complete greenhouse to go airborne at times, particularly warmer greenhouses that employ polycarbonate glazing. Make sure that it is securely stitched down to prevent this from happening. The mine is built on a steel basis, on which the dirt lies; nonetheless, each corner has a substantial amount of concrete poured into it. It has never gone any farther.

Protection of greenhouses from projectiles carried by the wind

So this is the technique to keep the end outside; but, what about objects that may potentially fly? It should go without saying that you should tidy up your garden before a storm hits. Put away or secure all of the yard equipment, including plant baskets, children's toys, and garden furniture. Glass may be broken by even fairly light objects that are carried by the wind, despite the fact that the wind's ability to toss large things about is incredible.

The fact that this does not prevent things from blowing in from any direction, however, means that there may be times when you need to actively protect your greenhouse. Some anglers, while fishing in areas with very strong winds, would surround their green houses with slatted wooden walls, end up, or hedges in order to filter out the end and also to redirect wind-borne items. This is done to protect their fish from being damaged. A disadvantage of this is that it may also reduce the overall quantity of light that reaches the plants within the greenhouse; nevertheless, if your greenhouse is located near a strong breeze tunnel or on a highly sensitive slope, a breeze barrier may prove to be quite useful.

Take some time after the strong winds have subsided to inspect your green-house when you get the opportunity. Be sure that all of the glazing clips are still in their places, firmly keeping the glazing in place, as there is a possibility that some of them might get dislodged and allow the glass to support itself. Cover any holes that have been created because panes have been lost or shattered until it is able to obtain replacements. Instead of using a simple sheet of vinyl, a tarpaulin, or even an outdated blanket to block the wind temporarily, you should use something far more effective such as the steps described above.

Everything that may possibly be grown in your greenhouse (veggies, fruits, herbs)

10 types of vegetable plants that you should think about growing

Producing plants in a greenhouse as starter plants or plant plants for customers to gather and grow is a completely different ball game than growing greenhouse vegetables for the purpose of harvesting the produce. Each may have its own own production issues, which you may not be accustomed to dealing with when working with decorative plants. However, each one possesses a substantial market potential with marketplaces that value and support local products, farm economies, local restaurant economies, and occasionally even your own retail performance.

There are not a lot of various types of produce plants that you are able to cultivate in the greenhouse, but the following are a few of the primary possibilities that you should look into if you are considering including vegetables into your own mix.

Inch. The use of rainwater to cultivate leafy greens, particularly salad types and bibb lettuces, is one of the most intriguing opportunities now available. There is a possibility that not all leafy greens will do well in the same conditions for growth that are necessary for the majority of ornamental plants, particularly plants. Because of this, the cosmetic business has to make very few adjustments in order to develop leafy vegetables. The only change that is necessary is the understanding of the evolving techniques for growing leafy greens, whether on land or in hydroponics. The sustainability has the potential to be remarkable provided that revenues are retained in the community and are distributed to customers in the most direct manner possible. There is a huge variety of greens available, each with its own distinct appearance, flavour, and texture. These days, it entails a great deal more than just a simple head of lettuce.

2. Microgreens are becoming increasingly popular in bars and restaurants. There is an incredible variety of microgreens, each with their own unique flavour. Each person has the ability to create their own unique blends of greens, which can then be used to offer a variety of flavours to diverse cuisines. Examples of unique micro-greens include things like persian cress, tatsoi, mustards, pac choi, radish, shungiku, amaranth, beet, orach, and so on. The not too distant future has a lot of promise!

3. Spinach is another another dark leafy green that has a favourable likelihood of survival. It used to be commercially sold and is now growing everywhere; it has a wonderful flavour. As a result of being grown in greenhouses, it is not only clean and devoid of waste and dirt but also sets an excellent standard for the safety of food. Due to the fact that it is grown in a greenhouse, it frequently goes to seed or bolts, and its age can be extremely advanced depending on the growth circumstances and the duration of the day.

4. Cucumbers are quite well-liked. Green onions are greenhouse kinds that some customers find more comfortable, but producing them might be a little bit more difficult because they need to be shrink-wrapped after they are harvested in order to keep them fresh and firm. The beit alpha types, which are becoming

increasingly popular, might be a superior option for younger children. I refer to them as "little snackers," and each of these little cucumbers is easy to pack because they do not need to be wrapped in plastic wrap like the European varieties need. Even the beit alpha types are soft, seedless, and tender, making them an excellent choice for packing in lunches at school.

5. Gone are the days of the most common and pleasant vegetable harvest from a greenhouse; today, there are a lot of unique options available in a wide variety of colours, forms, and hues. Popular options include beefsteaks, cherries, berries that are ripened on the vine (also known as tov), and other fruit. Many of the manufacturers that I work with are putting more of an emphasis on beef steak types. This is because the tov shapes are quite popular with some of the most significant growers who dominate the business.

6. Peppers continue to be another common crop harvested from greenhouses. Cake is a popular dessert in the United States, and consumers have a wide variety of options to choose from. Bell peppers grown in greenhouses require a humidity controller and certain levels of humidity. The best humidity controllers are from Holland. They have a flavour that is genuinely unparalleled, but growing them in a greenhouse is the most difficult harvest possible. On the other hand, there are many various varieties of peppers, each with their own distinct appearance, colour, and flavour. One day soon, grape vines will probably be supplied as edible ornamentals, delivering beauty in your home and also having the potential to be used to flavour a variety of food meals. In spite of these production challenges, peppers should prove to be a very marketable crop in the end. In addition to being enticing, the peppers in a clam shell come in a variety of hues.

7. A wide variety of herbs are available, and they can be packaged in a variety of different ways, either without or with the origins. Farmers are quickly discovering new plant species such as basil, water cress, cilantro, and countless more. These plants have a great future in plantation marketplaces, at which earnings may be led to the user, allowing for warmth and superbly excellent quality. These markets are expected to grow significantly in the coming years.

8. Green beans that have been cultivated in greenhouses have been in high demand, particularly in the inner city, leading to tremendous buying prices for these beans. Once more, customers have the option of purchasing a wide range of colours, in addition to a wide variety of forms and patterns. This really is a wonderful harvest for sales made directly to customers at farm economics.

9. Swiss chard and pineapple are both fantastic possibilities for production in greenhouses and should be marketed directly to the consumer. These two types of vegetables, like the vast majority of other vegetable plants, come in a wide variety of sizes, colours, and forms.

10. You won't have to go far to get strawberries, blueberries, and other berries cultivated in greenhouses. It is a success if production was boosted and it functioned with all of the shortcake on the manufacturing site. Why isn't it ever included as part of a person's offering in the farming sector when it's such an incredible deal at Wimbledon? If you want berries with the finest flavour, look for ones that are completely red all the way through and avoid buying them from suppliers located hundreds of kilometres away. The most delicious ones are now perishable, but they provide incredible opportunities if they are prepared locally.

Your greenhouse can support the growth of a variety of crops.

After the rainwater collection system and the necessary equipment have been installed, there is the possibility of cultivating vegetables. This will not actually add up to any more money than you would require for a rainwater collection system anyhow.

To begin, it is possible for you to cultivate varieties of fruit that would not have a chance of survival in the wild in the United Kingdom. Recent references have been made to bananas and pineapples; but, in addition to these, we are able to include the uncountable other kinds of citrus fruits (oranges, lemons etc.).

After that, you will come across the fruits that are just on the cusp of effectively maturing their exterior. They live in the open air, and during a good summer, they produce harvests that are satisfactory; however, they perform significantly better when housed in the protected environment of a greenhouse for the majority or a portion of the year. These are typically fruits such as grapes, nectarines and apricots, figs, grapes, and melons. Because, to tell you the truth, kiwi fruit, also known as Chinese gooseberries, have been far from the victor in competitions held outside of the southern region of the United Kingdom, we should absolutely include them among those. In point of fact, the only people who actually cultivate them are the proprietors of big heated greenhouses from the Channel Islands; many people gave up cultivating tomatoes in order to do this.

Aside from the kiwis, which may be implanted from the soil in the greenhouse, the other plants might be implanted in the margins of the greenhouse or in baskets so that they can be transported in less than very important times of the season but still remain outdoors. It's possible that this method will allow us to increase the list to include our very own incredibly hardy apples, pears, plums, and cherries.

Last but not least, the rainfall may be used to produce fruit outside of season, which might imply either late or early depending on the situation. The fruit known as the strawberry is a great example of this category.

Fruit tree orchards

Unfortunately, genuine exotics call for very specific conditions in order to thrive, and the gardener may not have the financial means to fulfil these criteria, particularly with relation to the heating system. However, provided that the frost can be kept outside and a little bit of additional warmth can be found, it is not difficult at all to produce citrus fruits. In point of fact, there is no reason why they should not be increased from fluctuation; however, you do face the same risk as you would with pears and apples. That is to say, it is quite unlikely that the progeny would be anything at all like the parent. As a result of this, rather than merely taking a chance, it is strongly recommended to acquire weapons from a reputable nursery rather than gambling on the purchase.

If you want to grow mature trees along the border of the greenhouse, the soil has to be well-drained and somewhat acidic. If you go ahead and plant them there, you'll have to take care of them. A limited number of vegetable crops benefit from the addition of extra soil.

Chapter Five

The trees

The John Innes Potting Mulch No. 3 is an excellent choice for the production of bud. Even a soil-based compost such as this is preferable to a peat mulch because it contributes significantly more equilibrium to the plant, and also the loam material functions as a tool of a buffer against sudden shifts in temperature and water content material. This makes a soil-based compost such as this preferable to a peat mulch. Clay containers are heavier than soil-based mulch, but this does not in any way make them more significant as a mulching material.

Peach trees and grape vines

It has been common practise for many centuries to harvest rainwater from trees in order to produce plants that are larger and of higher quality. This strategy is often applied to types of fresh fruit that are happy growing outside. There was not a big mansion everywhere that did not have a cherry tree in addition to a grapevine growing under glass. Both of these features were common. There is a good chance that they will be given the run of a full greenhouse for their own personal development. Peaches, nectarines, and apricots were typically fan-trained into the wall supporting lean-to structures in the rear of these homes. These structures were known as leanto houses. This may still be seen in some of the older and bigger country houses, despite the fact that the phenomenon is gradually becoming less common with each passing year. Many are replaced with plants like as tomatoes, which are then frequently sold in order to offset some of the ever-increasing costs that they face.

Grapes and berries, on the other hand, are quite popular, and there is no longer any reason why they shouldn't be grown in any greenhouse other than the smallest one. To give you an idea, you will need a space that is 6 feet square foot (4 square metres) in order to house a tree that is trained with a fan.

Now, grapes are frequently planted beyond the greenhouse and then led through a hole in the walls before being trained into the roofing. While this is not the best method because the very best growth begins growing until the origins in the spring, it does leave the greenhouse boundary free for other plants, such as berries. However, using growing bags for your own berries is not only going to make the process lot simpler, but it will also allow the vine to be planted within the bag.

Grapes aren't overly picky about the sort of soil they grow in; nonetheless, it should be well-drained and include a lot of organic material. A good way to do this is to build a planting position that is 3 feet square foot (1 square metre) in size and also 3 feet deep (1 metre). Although planting should ideally take place in the spring, it may also be done in the fall and during any light periods that occur throughout the winter.

Herb growing in green houses

Using a greenhouse gives you more control over the temperature, humidity, and light exposure that the plants receive, making it possible to create the optimal environment for plant growth. Growing herbs in a greenhouse offers the possibility of shielding sensitive annuals from the harsh heat of summer, so elongating the growing season and enabling the plants to mature earlier and later during the summertime. Setting up the greenhouse before putting in even a single plant is the optimal strategy for getting the most out of the space provided by the greenhouse. Installing a misting system and automatic trickle pads will ensure that your plants receive an adequate amount of moisture on a consistent basis. There are many reasons why herbs become neglected, but a lack of moisture is one of the most typical reasons. When you choose an automated system that provides a consistent, modest amount of water each day, you will be able to be confident that your plants will continue to grow over time. A method of planting plants is still another important component for the successful cultivation of herbs in greenhouses. Do not construct a roof for your brand-new greenhouse out of glass or plexi glass in its whole if you are going to be building it from the ground up. Some skylights or even sunroof-type installations are great for air movement, but most flowers need to have their branches pruned because of the bright sunlight during the day. In the event that your rainwater is collected, you may install it into the roofing by constructing a colour system using rip stop hooks, nylon, or velcro. In response to the needs of your plants, it will not be difficult to modify or eliminate this strategy at any time.

Herb varieties suitable for growing in greenhouses

The best herbs for expansion in a greenhouse are fragile annuals that are either too sensitive to grow in a normal garden or another herb that you would want to develop more vigorously and for a longer period of time than is typical for that herb. The following are examples of common herbs that may be cultivated in a greenhouse:

· basil

chives; chives

· cilantro

· d ill

· parsley

· chamomile

Due to the fact that mint is an invasive plant, it is imperative that it be grown in a container at all times. Despite this fact, mint is an excellent crop for farmers to cultivate. If you grow your mint in a greenhouse, you will have the opportunity to sample all of the myriad different types of mint that are available to home gardeners.

Growing plants throughout the year and learning how to properly schedule them for the year

How can you ensure that your garden greenhouse continues to provide food throughout the year? When you are organising the planting schedule for your greenhouse, the temperature and the length of the days are two of the most important factors to take into consideration.

When deciding whether or not to plant in your greenhouse, the day length is by far the most crucial factor to consider. If you aren't making use of any additional lighting, it is quite necessary for you to have a solid understanding of the typical day lengths that prevail in the area during the course of each season. In our part of Colorado, the beginning of old February is the period when our day span begins to exceed 10 hours each day; at this point, there is sufficient day light for seedlings to begin to grow. Around the middle of November, the number of days we have drops below 10 months, and the development of plants begins to slow down considerably. Plants are able to continue living through the winter months; however, they will often enter a semi-hibernation state during this time. If you start planting for winter early, your plants will probably be nearing maturity by the end of November, and you will be able to quickly harvest all winter from the semi-dormant plants without having to repaint the lights. If you plant for summer early, your plants will probably not be nearing maturity until the beginning of March.

The temperature in your greenhouse and the myriad of microclimates that exist within it can both have an effect on the plant's ability to flourish. The areas of your greenhouse that are closest to a greenhouse gas and to your vents will often be the ones with the lowest temperatures. During the winter, you should plant cold-hardy veggies like kale and spinach in this location since it will be the most beneficial for their growth. The part of your greenhouse that is connected with the north wall will typically be the hottest since sunlight will bounce off of this wall and hit the plants that are located in this location. You will be able to harvest vegetables throughout the year if you organise your planting programme according to the length of the day, adjust the location of your plants according to the temperature, and select the plants and kinds that are best for your climate.

The following is a rigorous putting calendar that we use for the site close to Denver, Colorado, which is around 40 degrees north latitude.

February:

As we all get closer to the equinox, we may notice that the days are beginning to get longer. In our part of Colorado, the month of February marks the beginning of the period during which there is an adequate amount of day light (about ten hours each day) to begin the process of seeding new crops without the need to make use of supplementary lighting.

Start cataloguing your very first spring planting of cold-hardy plants so you can use them later (lettuce, kale, radishes, beets, carrots, peas, and so forth).

In the greenhouse, you should start storing warm-loving and long-season vegetable plants (berries, peppers, eggplant, and so forth). Because these plants take an average of 100–150 weeks to mature and because they typically cannot survive the winter, we want to ensure that we provide them with the longest possible period of time in a comfortable growth environment while they are maturing and developing their fruit. You can start these plants in your own greenhouse, and then once the nighttime temperatures have consistently been over 55 degrees, you can move them outside to finish growing. Alternately, you'll have the option of letting them continue to climb on your greenhouse all the way through the summer and into the fall.

March/april:

When we get closer to the spring equinox, the days start to become longer, and the plants in the greenhouse start to develop more quickly. Start planting seeds for warm-season plants that reach maturity in fewer days (legumes, basil, cucumbers, squash).

Start harvesting the first round of cold-resistant plants, and while you're doing it, keep planting more cold-resistant plants that are fast growing to replace the ones you just harvested.

Might:

The days are becoming longer, and the nights are getting warmer, which allows for considerably quicker growth in your greenhouse.

It is very likely that you will be picking a significant amount of food from plants such as lettuce, spinach, and beans.

If you have begun defecating outside the greenhouse, then you are now able to start planting cold rancid transplants outside (lettuce, cabbage, cauliflower) once the evening temperatures have been always above 4.5 degrees, and you can begin planting hot summer transplants outside (berries, peppers, eggplant) at once the night temperatures have been always above 55 degrees. If you have begun defecating inside the greenhouse, then you are now able to begin planting hot summer transplants outside (peppers, eggplant

June/july:

Depending on the type of cooling systems that you have, this is typically the warmest time of year for greenhouses. Your warm-loving plants, such as berries, eggplant, beans, and berries, will thrive in the greenhouse; however, you will still need to monitor the temperature to prevent it from becoming too high and ensure that there is adequate ventilation and humidity to prevent the plants from drying out too quickly and wilting. (if you want to learn more about the relationship between the humidity and temperatures in your greenhouse, check see our page all about vpd.)

August/september:

August and September are typically the months in which you start planting your winter crops. The days are shorter from November through January, which means that plants will develop extremely slowly without any additional light if they don't get it. If you want to have a successful cold garden, you need to start planting your seeds as early as possible so that your plants will be close to reaching maturity by November or perhaps December. Because plant development slows down, your plants will go into a "hibernation" that is semi-permeable, and you will be able to harvest slowly over the course of winter without having to visit very fresh growth. This is because your plants will go into a semi-permeable "hibernation."

Before your region's first frost is also the time to relocate a few potted plants inside the greenhouse to winter storage for the season. Citrus, figs, peppers, and berries that are grown outside in pots have a chance of surviving the winter in the greenhouse if the containers are moved inside. We have just discovered pepper plants in containers that have been nurtured in this manner for more than three years and are still bearing fruit.

October:

The number of daylight hours has begun to decrease. You have now established your winter garden, but October can still provide sufficient lighting to start very short cycle plants (such as radishes, which only need 20-30 days to grow), or even to start

plants that you intend to harvest from the late winter/early spring, even though you are aware that their growth will be very sluggish throughout the duration of winter. For example, radishes require only 20-30 days to grow.

When hardy vegetables such as spinach, lettuce, and lettuce are planted now, they will normally have enough time to germinate and eventually become little plants, survive the winter, and develop quickly once February arrives because the days become longer. Due to the fact that vegetables begin to store sugars inside their cell walls during the winter and early spring, the taste of vegetables during these seasons of the year is sweeter than at other times of the year.

November/december/january:

A time for rest and hibernation that comes just before the start of another season. Pulling kale leaves, grinding carrots and beets, or chopping lettuce are all examples of activities that may be used to continue harvesting produce from plants that are getting on in years. In addition, this is the time of year to get your hands dirty by trimming your fruit trees, perusing seed catalogues, and making other preparations for the next year's garden.

In the event that you want to make use of supplementary illumination, the growth of your greenhouse plants does not have to slow down during this period of time. With just a little bit of extra light, leafy greens and fruits may thrive throughout the winter and summer months. When nighttime temperatures in the greenhouse can remain at or above 62 degrees, we've seen cold greenhouses successfully cultivate warm-season plants like tomatoes and berries with the use of additional lighting. Because a ceres greenhouse is able to gather light coming in from all directions, including the north, west, and west sides of the structure, we are able to utilise less supplementary light while still achieving robust growth during the winter.

6 essential guidelines for newcomers to the practise of growing plants in greenhouses

Growing your own food in a greenhouse is a highly satisfying and enjoyable pastime; but, the learning curve may be rather steep, just like it is with any other activity that requires a certain amount of knowledge and expertise. Even when growing the vast majority of plant species, there is truly a large number of elements that might effect growth rates as well as the consequences of a return. These factors include:

Chapter Six

Tips

It might be challenging to get everything right on your very first season if you are new to rainwater harvesting. While mistake and try is an equally important part of the learning process, these six pointers provide any farmers a head start.

1. Planting seeds according to the season

You may even get a head start on spring and summer by cultivating specific vegetables all through the year in a greenhouse, which is one of the most significant benefits of owning a greenhouse. Another significant advantage is that you can extend the growing seasons. Our growing guide gives you a terrific insight into what items should be planted when, but once you start organising your successful programme, it is essential that you stock up on the essential seed starting materials you'll need to obtain a powerful return on your investment. You must need to buy at the very least:

Containers

Sterile soil (essential to reduce the risk of pest disease and infections)

Fertiliser

Water

Additionally, we suggest that you invest in heating resources in order to facilitate the dispersal of seeds at the beginning of the summer season, when temperatures are still relatively mild. Even if there are extra methods such as heating wires hidden in seed seats, a propagation heating pad is one of the most economical and straightforward ways to warm seed apartments and boost development. Another option is to use heating cables.

2. The origins of light

A swallow or e-lite greenhouse ought to get adequate natural illumination for your plants throughout the late summer and spring months; however, if you want to grow during the late fall and winter months, a supplemental lighting system is required if you want your plants to be healthy and robust.

One of the most often utilised types of lighting is high definition lamp strips and led grow lights. This is due to the fact that, in contrast to other types of lighting systems, such as crystal spectrum lighting, they have become more energy efficient and can also cover a larger area.

A normal fluorescent strip that is suspended 37 inches above the plants may commonly degrade whether you are cultivating a larger harvest or are cultivating a smaller crop in a small and more cost-effective greenhouse.

3. Getting hotter

The process of learning how to heat a greenhouse during the warmer months may be an educational experience in and of itself. People who are not accustomed to growing plants in rainwater can consider utilising electric heaters because they are less difficult to install, more affordable, and come in a wider variety of software options. Even a simple heater that operates at 120 volts may adequately heat a small greenhouse, but bigger greenhouses require a heater that operates at 240 volts or more and is managed by a thermostat that is both dependable and waterproof.

The performance of gas heaters is comparable to that of electric heaters; however, gas heaters have a reputation for being more cost-effective. In addition, gas heaters require a steady supply of air for combustion and also a means of fume fatigue.

Creating ventilation systems that utilise unwanted warm air and expel it from your home is an example of a less energy-intensive kind of heating that may appeal to consumers who are concerned about the environment. Many companies who produce their goods in relatively modest-sized greenhouses also make use of heat-absorbing materials, such as huge stones and other types of substances, which soak up the sun's rays throughout the day and then gradually give off that heat when the sun sets. These procedures are an excellent approach for maintaining a constant temperature within the greenhouse over the course of the day, even when supplementary heating equipment is being utilised.

4. Chilling out

Even during the height of summer, it could be difficult to keep a greenhouse at a steady temperature in the United Kingdom, despite the fact that the climate there is generally more mild. It is considerably more difficult to bring down the temperature in a greenhouse that has been excessively hot than it is to bring up the temperature in a greenhouse that is too chilly. Greenhouses are purpose-built to maintain and retain heat.

Because of this, taking the temperature inside the greenhouse or potting shed on a consistent and regular basis throughout the warmer months is of the utmost importance. Taking regular temperature readings might be the difference between being able to adjust the temperature in the greenhouse merely by opening the door and having to make use of an artificial cooling system. If your rainwater has a habit of making loud snoring noises, we suggest installing evaporative air jets, which keep the humidity level steady.

5. Providing air circulation in a greenhouse

The changing of the seasons plays a significant part in determining the size of any greenhouse. Convection currents are created by the pure heat during the summer, and there are sufficient amounts of them to maintain good flow. During the summer, if you leave the vents in either the walls or the roof open, chilly air will be drawn in via the walls, while hot air will flow through the roof, ensuring that there is a steady supply of oxygen.

However, during the winter months it may be more difficult to maintain adequate air movement and to stop the growth of mould. Even while it may help a great deal to prevent the soil from being overly saturated with water, most greenhouse manufacturers ensure that an oscillating fan is operating during the bulk of the winter months.

6. Giving the plants water to drink

The practise of watering plants in accordance with a group schedule is one of the most common and one of the most common blunders that beginning farmers do. There are quite a few aspects that determine whether or not plants require mowing. These factors include humidity, temperature, and the growth stage of the plants themselves. The development stage of the plants has a significant impact on how much water will be required.

Throughout the middle of winter, you might only need to water a seed seat once every ten weeks, but during the summer, you should probably increase the frequency of your waterings. Quantifying the amount of moisture in the soil, either with a moisture metre or just by looking at the appearance and feel of the soil, is the best approach for determining whether or not the plants require further watering at a given time.

Taking care of your greenhouse's upkeep and cleaning it

Why do you insist on sterilising your greenhouse?

It is essential to clean the greenhouse on a consistent basis or once each year in order to avoid unwanted pests and illnesses from entering. Insects are able to grow or overwinter in this safe habitat, which, in addition to bolstering plant health, provides the optimum circumstances for these activities. It is likely that plant infections will continue to exist in the earth, algae will grow from the traces, and also gnats will reproduce on natural deposits. Insects and germs will coagulate in crevices and gaps.

Performing a methodical cleaning of your greenhouse.

Plants

Inch. Find a time of year when the weather is more favourable for a few of days and drain the seas of all plant materials, including any weeds that seek to get a foothold on tiled flooring. Do this during a period when the weather is more favourable for longer.

2. Keep an eye out for any existing insects or illnesses, and use a mulch made from plants that are susceptible to such problems.

3. Perform a thorough inspection of any citrus or tropical plants you have, looking for increasing species of scale, mealybugs, whiteflies, or even spider mites. Before the issue is resolved entirely, apply precautionary techniques of guidance and isolate the affected area. You may learn more by reading the post we wrote on spider mites, which explains how to naturally control them and detect them.

Pots and methods

1. Clean all components of the greenhouse, including trays, baskets, and other apparatus, with warm water and let them sit in a solution of water bleach

consisting of three-quarters of a cup of chlorine bleach to one gallon of potable water.

2. Recycle or dispose of the disposable seed trays and baskets, and move them as far away from the greenhouse as feasible whenever you can.

Soils

Chapter Seven

Conclusions

Pathogens such as pythium, fusarium, rhizoctonia, fungus gnats, grubs, root aphids, and many more may be present on old lands. It is recommended that lands be removed from beds and baskets, and that mulch be left in place for an additional year or two.

In the spring or just before planting a fresh harvest, replace the old oil with new oil that has not been contaminated with illness and that was purchased from a reputable provider. This includes the soil that is on your baskets and beds as well as the dirt that is between the chairs on the walkways and under them.

To remove any debris, either remove it carefully or sweep it up, and then, at the conclusion of the washing process, when the rainfall is likely to be sitting, care for the entire exposed region with all of the soil.

Irrigation

Purge harmful bacteria from hauling and irrigation tanks. In addition to fostering the growth of algae, irrigation lines and carrying tanks almost definitely play host to tens of thousands of gnats, which pose a risk to individual hair follicles. After adding three quarters of a cup of oxygen bleach to one gallon of hot water, you should flush any traces, remove any dripper heads, and wash away carrying tanks any residue from fertilisers.

Structure in addition to wood

Inch. The structure of the greenhouse provides an excellent sanctuary for insects that choose to overwinter there. Greenhouses with metal structure are not particularly vulnerable, but they still need to be disinfected. Wood is the most effective material for giving spider mites, thrips, aphids, and whitefly with the right crevices and cracks that they utilise as a hiding place. Wood also has the most cracks.

2. Use an air cleaning solution to thoroughly clean the rainwater glass and the structure it is attached to.

3. Coat all of the exposed wood with horticultural oil that is derived from vegetables. This is done with a brush to ensure that the oil gets into any gaps in order to smother any bacteria that may be hiding there.

4. Give the farmers the option to go into hibernation throughout the winter, if at all feasible. Make sure that washed earth is used to replace the plants that were previously there and to only show plants that are disease and pest free.

Ongoing maintenance and cleaning of the greenhouse

Inch. Avoiding practises like as pruning, planting, or inter-cropping all during the growing season can help reduce the risk of problems migrating from one harvest to the next.

2. Deal with "green branches" or weeds and volunteer plants as quickly as possible since they have the potential to act as hosts for diseases that are spread between plants.

3. Remove from the growing area any plants that are known to spread illnesses or harbour intestinal bugs as soon as you become aware of them. Not only will this prevent the disease from spreading, but it will also make it much simpler to clean up.

4. Avoid recontamination. Fleas and infections can be transferred from one location to another on newly acquired items of clothes, footwear, and plants.

5. Always observe proper hygiene, and after touring the potentially hazardous components of the greenhouse, refrain from returning there at a later time.

6. Make it a habit to regularly clean your equipment and wash any jars that are going to be reused. The more effort you put into anything, the more potential for harm there is.

What kind of care is required for a greenhouse?

First, conduct a thorough cleaning of the greenhouse. Stage 1

When is the soonest that I should clean my greenhouse?

If you intend to utilise your greenhouse throughout the whole year, you should give it a thorough cleaning at the beginning of each growing season.

2. Conduct a thorough inspection of the greenhouse panels

Examine the glass panes that make up the greenhouse's glazing in great detail. In the case that you found any of those panels to be broken or cracked, you should replace those panels.

Stage 3 — search for slipping greenhouse panels

In most cases, the panels are mounted upon putty or glue, and they are kept in place with propane brads embedded in the wooden structure.

Phase 4: Examine the structure of the greenhouse

The many components of the framework each require their own maintenance check list. Now I'm going to concentrate on just two of their agricultural possibilities, although both of them are highly popular: aluminium and aluminium.

Phase 5: Continue to operate from a greenhouse base

The present moment is ideally suited for inspecting the base of your greenhouse. During a thorough cleaning, make sure that it is as empty as it is possible to get it.

Phase 6: Pay attention to the ventilation in the greenhouse

The establishment of a safe environment for the plants is significantly aided by the provision of adequate ventilation. You may have the option of installing either manual or automated port openers on your greenhouse.

When the temperature inside becomes uncomfortable, an automatic opener might be attached to the vents or windows so that they open on their own.

Step Seven: Investigate Possible Methods of Shading Greenhouses

When the temperature outside becomes too high during the summer months, shading will protect your crops from being damaged. In order to save money on the glazing, the gardener decided to utilise outdated mesh curtains, roll-up colours, and plastic.

Phase 8 — greenhouse door replacements

You have the option of installing either hinged or sliding doors on your greenhouse. Both kinds of gateways are convenient.

Controlling pests in the greenhouse is the focus of Phase 9.

Ohmygod! Controlling pests may be a real pain in the neck (personal experience). These itty-bitty critters will resort to whatever means necessary in order to consume your plants.

Tips and advice on how to cut down on expenses.

How to save money while shopping at nurseries and garden supply stores

Have you been unable to contain your excitement about getting your new backyard and landscaping? Getting started? A trip to your community gardening or angling centre may be in order if you want to make the most of this time of year, which is an ideal time to give your yard its finest appearance of the year. This is the location where the majority of your planting materials, such as plants, bark, and many other things, will be found. There are ways to cut costs while going to these centres; I will list five of them below for your convenience. Have a look at some inventive methods on how to spend less money in green houses and gardening centres, which will enable you to have your yard looking beautiful for less money.

The method for reducing expenditures in gardening centres and greenhouses

Inch. Carry out just a little bit of cyberstalking.

It's possible that this will make you laugh, but it's actually a terrific method to get some additional discounts! Have a look at the website of your preferred gardening centre. Find both their Facebook page and their website. If they provide any discounts over the internet, such as a mailing list or coupons that can be printed out, then this is the section where you will be able to find that information. You could also be able to learn about forthcoming events and sales if you take advantage of this opportunity.

2. Focus on the details.

It is tempting to choose plants that are older and larger; nevertheless, doing so will result in a significantly higher investment on your part. Alternately, you might go with seedlings and starter plants that are of a lesser size. You may buy them for just one dollar each, and in a very short amount of time, they will quickly become robust and substantial on their own. Your perseverance may be rewarded.

3. You shouldn't be afraid of plant material that has been used previously.

Some crops could be disregarded if they have a drab appearance and a scraggly appearance. Ask yourself if it is possible to store plants in such a state. Is it possible that only a little bit of fertiliser and some trimming would be sufficient? Would the beginnings be good for you? In the event that this is the case, you should rescue these neglected plants and tend to them.

4. Request a discount.

This may come out as audacious, but it is effective nonetheless. In the event that you come across a plant or a shrub that you like, but it is damaged or perhaps it is the last one in store, inquire as to whether or not it is possible to return it. In addition, you have the option of inquiring about price reductions if you are purchasing in large quantities or if your purchase is being made on behalf of a charitable organisation such as a church or playground.

5. Make sure to purchase locally grown plants.

The plants, such as lilies, might be interesting; but, given that they are not native to the area, the expense of purchasing them is going to be higher. Choose plants that are native to both your location and the surrounding area. Not only are these plants more likely to thrive, but they also have a better chance of being significantly more affordable.

CPSIA information can be obtained
at www.ICGtesting.com
Printed in the USA
LVHW081319060922
727596LV00030B/612